A Catholic Bishop

Brothers and Sisters in Christ: A Catholic Teaching on the Issue of Immigration

Most Reverend Nicholas DiMarzio

BASILICA ™

P R E S S

Published by
Basilica Press
III Ferguson Court, Ste. 102
Irving, TX 75062

Editor: David Uebbing
Cover Design: Giuliana Gerber/ACI Prensa
Layout: Cheryl Vaca

Printed in the United States of America
ISBN 978-1930314248

Basilica Press is part of the Joseph and Marie Daou Foundation.

TABLE OF CONTENTS

1) Isn't immigration a political and legal topic? Why should the Church involve itself in this matter?

Immigration is a political topic, just as the abortion issue is if you want to look at it from that point of view. It is something that is debated in the country and something that prompts the passing of laws to regulate it. The Church involves itself in this matter, however, because there is moral content, as in most issues of public policy. Society's failure to obey the Gospel imperative to "welcome the stranger" is manifested in numerous ways. We are implicated by policies that lead to migrant crossing deaths, that separate families, that deny protection to those fleeing violence and intense privation, that exploit people in the workforce, and that expose people to unconscionable conditions of confinement, including children.

The Church has been involved in the immigration issue since the birth of the nation. The Church is an immigrant church that has grown through the new blood of immigrants. It has a long history of integrating immigrants into their new land. As a universal organization present in sending communities, the Church has a full understanding of what compels migrants to come here. As a result, it has a lot to say about the immigration issue and enrich the public debate in this regard.

2) Is there any moral issue involved in the immigration debate?

Yes, the moral issue is the dignity of the human person, which is the basis of all Catholic social teaching. The dignity of the human person prompts us to defend the right to life from conception to natural death. It also prompts Catholics to defend the fair treatment of all persons who are in our country, whether they be illegal, or, as I prefer to say, in undocumented status. By any fair reckoning, many of today's migrants are forced to uproot by conditions, whether political or economic, that are not worthy of human dignity. This analogy is hardly exact, but the issue can be compared to slavery two centuries ago. Slavery was defended as a moral right, and yet we know how wrong that conception was. In our own day, the treatment of aliens without legal status in our country is similar to the public debate on slavery and makes Catholics take a moral position on immigration. The issue of immigration is complex. There are many specific policy questions that are matters of prudential judgment where disagreement may occur. The preservation of the dignity of the human person, however, must be the guiding principle. Whenever some particular immigration law disregards that basic human right to fair treatment, careful consideration must be given to the position taken.

The Church has first hand knowledge that the current immigration system undermines the human dignity of the person, and, in some cases, threatens human life. Our social service programs, hospitals, and schools, not to mention our parishes, see the human consequences of a broken system. People are exploited, abused, separated from their families, and even die in the desert. The system must be changed to ensure that people can migrate in a safe, controlled, and humane manner.

3) Can Catholics rightfully disagree on the issue of immigration?

The issue of immigration is a complex social policy question and finds Catholics in legitimate disagreement. However, Catholics cannot be on either side of the principle that should guide our consideration on this issue, that is, the dignity and life of the human person. As stated previously, it is the basis of all Catholic social teaching. Catholics may disagree on particulars; but each Catholic must judge themselves on the issue of how well their immigration position upholds human dignity and human life.

For example, enforcement techniques that drive migrants into remote parts of the desert or into the hands of smugglers should be reviewed. Detention policies that separate families, as well as enforcement raids, should be carefully scrutinized to determine whether the violation of human dignity can be eradicated. The U.S. Bishops believe that the most humane path to preserve the dignity of the person is through comprehensive immigration reform.

4) Can a Catholic rightfully be opposed to the presence of immigrants in our country?

Truly, it would be throwback to the restrictionist policies of the 19th and 20th Centuries when Asians, as well as Southern and Eastern Europeans (who were mostly Catholics) were restricted from our country on the basis of racial and ethnic discrimination. As a nation of immigrants, it would be foolhardy to think that barring immigrants permanently from our country would be in the national interest. It certainly would go against our national heritage as a nation of immigrants. Our Catholic social principles tell us that all persons have a right to migrate to find work and support their families. At the same time, we also know that every country has a right to admit or refuse migrants. These rights must be balanced by the common good. So moral choices are necessary to balance what a country can offer to immigrants and, indeed, what the immigrants themselves can offer.

The Bishops are trying to advance reform of the current system so that immigrants can enter our country legally and have legal status, which would help protect their God-given rights.

5) Can Catholics rightfully be opposed to any kind of immigration, even legal?

Immigration has become a structural reality in most industrialized nations' in social policies. It has also become a world-wide phenomenon. It would be almost impossible in the globalized world to restrict immigration. At the same time, it would also be against our Catholic social teaching to restrict immigration for self-serving purposes.

For those who would call for a moratorium or a complete ban on any kind of immigration, one should look at ones own family history and how their ancestors came to be here in the United States. If this was the policy of our nation from its inception, none of us would be here, except the Native Americans. We should also recall our own biblical heritage. From the Exodus to the Exile period, from the Holy Family's flight into Egypt, to the itinerant ministry of Jesus, to the travels of St. Paul and our Church's early missionaries, we have always been a Church of migrants. Given this tradition and the fact that we are a global Church, it would be very odd for us, to say the least, to oppose any kind of immigration.

6) In the case of illegal immigration, shouldn't Catholics side with the law?

Illegal immigration is not something condoned by the Church. In our tradition, however, laws must be just. In this regard, an analogy might be drawn to another contentious social policy issue; namely, that of abortion. If Catholics were to side with the law permitting abortion, it would be an immoral act. And so it is with immigration laws when they do not respect the dignity of the human person, nor reflect Catholic social teaching. Laws are man made and all laws are not equally just. There are times when Catholics are asked to work for the change of laws, while at the same time obeying laws where the rights of conscience are not violated. For example, in 1996 a change in immigration laws prohibited permanent resident aliens from receiving the same benefits as citizens, such as food stamps. At that time, a benefit intended to ensure proper nourishment for the families of low-income workers excluded these low and entry-level workers. It seems that there was a question of moral fairness about this misguided policy. Siding with a law permitting abortion helps promote an immoral act and siding with an unjust immigration law also promotes an immoral act.

7) Most of the recent immigrants have come to the country in violation of the law; so shouldn't they be regarded as criminals?

Immigration violations have traditionally been enforced as "civil" laws, although more and more they are being turned into crimes and prosecuted as such. Most immigrants, however, are not criminals in any standard sense of the term. Most simply want to work hard, provide for their families and practice their faith. We must go beyond the issue of law here to find out what motivates immigrants to come to our country. What one finds is that it is mostly the lack of opportunity at home and the greater availability of opportunities here. The fact that one breaks a law, of course, also begs the question of the severity of the crime and the proportionality of the punishment. The U.S. Bishops recognize that the law has been broken, but favor allowing undocumented immigrants to earn the right to remain through their hard work, their good character and learning English.

We must consider the *intent* and the *effect* of the law breaking to ascertain the penalty. The intent of the migrant is to work and help their families, and the effect, from our view and many others, is that they help our economy by working in important industries. These factors should mitigate the penalty, such as paying a fine or any taxes owed.

If it were known that certain immigrants were here illegally, wouldn't it be immoral to provide them with any kind of help? And wouldn't it be even more immoral to grant them permanent residency or citizenship?

Assisting persons, be they undocumented citizens or permanent residents, should not be conditioned by their legal status in the United States. Instead, we should assist people in response to the injunction in Matthew 25, "When I was a stranger you welcomed me." Basic human assistance is a matter of Christian charity. Certainly, it would not be immoral to grant permanent residency or citizenship to those who find themselves here in undocumented status. This has been a part of the immigration law practically since its inception. For example, ship jumpers were always given the possibility of regularizing their status. Until some recent changes in the law, people who immigrated to the U.S. were given a "registry date," and if they maintained a record free of any criminal activity, they were normally able to adjust their status. Current law dictates that anyone in the U.S. since 1972 is allowed to become legalized. It has always been a part of the immigration system to allow those who

find themselves here in undocumented status to regular-
ize their status.

8) Shouldn't Catholics be concerned about immigrants taking jobs that belong to Americans?

The issue of displacement, that is, of immigrants taking the jobs that belong to Americans, is a complex one. The first question is, "Who is an American?" America belongs as much to the person who became a citizen yesterday as to the one whose family has been here for several hundred years. This is what makes our society great. Everyone is able to call themselves an American as they become part of our society. It may be true that there is displacement in certain sectors of our labor market. Studies show that undocumented immigrants do compete with Americans without a high school diploma, which is about 12 percent of the workforce. Displacement, however, is a factor no matter what the legal status of an immigrant might be. There is always displacement in the labor market, but there is always room for more workers that expand the economy.

Overwhelmingly, immigrants, undocumented or otherwise, *complement* the American labor force, not *displace* it. They perform jobs in industries that are important to our economy--agriculture, construction, service, as well as highly skilled professionals-- that depend on their contributions. In addition, immigrant laborers will be needed even more as our 79 million strong Baby Boomer generation begins to retire.

9) **Shouldn't Catholics be concerned about immigrants taking jobs that belong to Americans? Shouldn't Catholics be concerned about America losing its identity on account of having too many immigrants?**

The identity of America is one that depends not on its racial or ethnic make-up, but rather its commitment to Democracy and certain values that have made us a great nation. There are certain xenophobic tendencies that believe that any alien will destroy the American identity, whatever that is held to be. Our history as a nation has taught us that the more open a society we have been, the greater progress has been made in forging and continually strengthening the American identity. Immigrants do not take away our culture, they help shape it.

10) Isn't it legitimate to be concerned about the burden that immigrants place on our economy and its system of services intended for our citizens?

There is no proof that immigrants place a burden on our economy. In fact, the evidence contradicts that claim. Immigrants are in reality a net gain, since they have been educated outside this country. They are no cost to our system and yet bring needed skills and education to the labor market. The same is true about the system of services intended for our citizens. Immigrants pay taxes as everyone else, billions of dollars each year in sales, property, and, yes, income taxes. In fact, they receive less in services than native-born people (e.g. Food Stamps). Undocumented immigrants are ineligible for federal benefits and only receive food stamps and TANF if there is a U.S. citizen child in the family. Thus, less than 1 percent of households headed by undocumented immigrants receive cash assistance, while 5 percent of households headed by U.S.-born citizens do. In addition, undocumented immigrants pay literally billions of dollars per year into the Social Security trust fund, most of which they may never be able to collect.

11) Should a Catholic report to the authorities the presence of an illegal immigrant? Would it be the moral thing to do?

There is no obligation in the law for any citizen to report the suspected legal status of an immigrant. Until such laws are passed, this would be an immoral thing to do, since it is going beyond what the law requires. It is also not at all easy to determine who is and is not undocumented. To provide just one example, several millions people in the United States have been approved for visas based on their close family relationship to a U.S. citizen or lawful permanent resident. Due to backlogs in our immigration system, many of these people must wait for years until their visas are available. Many accuse the undocumented of trying to jump ahead of the line by trying to immigrate to the United States, however, the fact of the matter is that millions of undocumented immigrants are already in the line. They already have been approved for a visa.

Overall, the basic premise of this question is a flawed one, since it equates every man-made law as equal to God's law. This is not true. Man makes flawed law all the time, because he is imperfect. The immigration law in the U.S. is very flawed. While we should still obey it, we have no obligation to go beyond its reach or even implement it on our own. Our moral obligation lies in changing the law to make it just.

12) If we were to change the laws to accommodate illegal immigrants, wouldn't we be weakening our legal system?

Changes in our immigration system that might legalize undocumented aliens would not weaken our legal system, but in fact strengthen the system. The 1986 Amnesty Program gave us an opportunity to strengthen our immigration system. The accommodation to accept new future flows of immigrants, however, was ignored, as well as work-force enforcement of the hiring of undocumented aliens.

The problem we face today is that our current system encourages illegality and, in fact, relies on it. While the desire for the cheap labor of an illegal workforce helps keep prices of goods low, sadly, we do not protect these worker's rights. What we need is an orderly, regulated system of immigration, not one characterized by illegality. The complete overhaul of the system is necessary. In fact, such a revamping would strengthen our immigration laws, not weaken them.

13) Wouldn't it be better to have illegal immigrants stay in their own countries?

The Church has always taught that a person has a right to remain in their home country, which means that they should have the jobs at home needed to support themselves and their families. However, this is not always possible because of the state of our world—a world in which some countries are much wealthier than others. The Church has always advocated that the best way to solve the issue of illegal immigration is to economically develop underdeveloped countries and provide jobs for migrants in their own communities. In fact, our overseas relief agency, Catholic Relief Services, supports several programs designed to allow people to remain at home. As has been repeated over and over again, undocumented immigration is neither good for our country, nor for the aliens themselves. The fact is, they are here because there is a need for their labor and because they can find work and earn ten times in a day what they would earn at home.

14) Why are some bishops opposing the building of a fence to prevent immigrants from coming in? Isn't it the moral right of a nation to protect its borders?

The U.S. bishops oppose the building of a fence to prevent immigrants from coming in to our country, because they recognize that the fence will not only be ineffective, but also it will put the lives of many who will cross the border in danger. Truly, every nation has a right to protect its border, however, the idea that a fence which is built by only one nation can protect a border that has two sides is ill-conceived. While it may slow down migration for a while, migrants will find a way around it, under it, over it, or through it because the forces that compel them to come are stronger than any fence. It would be much better if the United States engaged Mexico, its neighbor to the South, in critical economic development opportunities in migrant-sending communities in Mexico, thus defending its borders from both sides. This would be a better way to protect our national sovereignty, and to respect the sovereignty of our neighbor to the South, our largest trading partner.

The other aspect of a fence is the signal it sends to the world. We are the world's greatest democracy—history shows that we are safer when we are open to the rest of the world and engage it.

15) Is there any circumstance in which it is morally imperative to accept immigrants in our country?

Many times, there is a moral imperative to accept refugees into our country, a sub-set of immigrants who are people fleeing persecution. There certainly is sufficient Church teaching to recognize that we should protect the lives of those who are most vulnerable, especially those fleeing persecution. As for economic migrants, countries should try to accommodate them to the degree that it furthers the common good. In the current situation, a generous immigration policy in the United States serves the common good.

16) **Is there any difference if the immigrants are Catholic? Should the local Catholics treat them any differently?**

Whether or not immigrants are Catholic should not change the way local Catholics treat them. They are human beings and we should treat all persons equally, with respect and dignity, not because they are Catholic but because we are Catholic.

17) Aren't immigrants placing a burden on our Catholic Church here in the United States?

The challenge of integrating new immigrants into the Catholic Church in the United States is an asset rather than a burden. Our immigrants bring new life and vitality to the Church, despite the challenges involved with adding new members. They are revitalizing our Church.

18) Aren't immigrants hurting their own countries by leaving?

The issue of immigrants leaving their home countries has commonly been known as the "brain drain" problem. Others see it as "brain circulation." The fact of the matter is, it is not brains that leave their home country, but rather human persons who make decisions. Many times, the difficult decision an immigrant makes, especially a highly-skilled immigrant, can have a temporary effect on their home country. But the sending of remittances, and sometimes the eventual return of these highly-qualified immigrants, can be a benefit to their home country instead of a loss.

19) **Most immigrant Catholics have their own traditions, don't tithe, and solicit services that local parishes find hard to provide. Doesn't that weaken our Church structures?**

Immigrant Catholics certainly have their own traditions and are not used to tithing to the same extent that the vast majority of American Catholics are used to doing. Despite what people think, immigrants seek no more services than others from the parishes. Eventually, they will become supporting Catholics as is seen in second-generation immigrants who integrate very well with the structures of the Church, and in fact support them for the future generations. Most of the structures and institutions that now characterize the Catholic Church in the United States came into being or grew dramatically during our nation's last great wave of immigrants from roughly 1890 to 1920, when 75 percent of all Catholics were foreign-born. These immigrants created the Church structures we now take for granted. I suspect our current immigrants will have a similarly positive effect.

20) **How do we balance the right of a person to have a better life with the right of a nation to protect its borders?**

The balance of the right of a person to have a better life and the right of a nation to protect its borders must be balanced by the common good. The common good knows no international boundaries. It must be the good of all that we must considered, the good of the immigrant and the person seeking a better life and nation, combined with that nation's ability to provide a good life. Countries have responsibility to their own populations and, in fact, openness to immigration, in most circumstances, strengthens the country instead of weakening it.

21) Hasn't immigration become a security issue since 9/11? Shouldn't Catholics be totally supportive of the effort to protect our borders?

Immigration truly has become a security issue, even prior to 9/11. Catholics should be supportive of the efforts to protect our borders; however, there is much discussion as to the best way to accomplish this goal. The problem of undocumented immigration and security is not a problem of our borders solely; it is a problem of our internal policies, most especially our labor market. Without some type of workplace enforcement and a secure identity card, it is my personal opinion, that we will never solve the immigration issue at the borders. But this must be achieved in a comprehensive immigration reform bill, which is the only way to make us truly secure. By legalizing the undocumented, we know who they are. By increasing the number of work visas for foreign-born workers to enter and work, we know who is coming into the country and we are better able to control the border.

22) What does the call to Christian charity ask of us when it comes to the immigration issue?

Christian charity asks of us, as we approach the immigration issue, that we understand the facts since we cannot direct our charity to any group without understanding the true situation. We can not listen to the voices of racist and nativist politicians, or media moguls, and expect to exercise Christian charity. We must look at the reality of the immigrants in our midst in order to form and direct our charity. We only need to look as far as Christ's instruction to us in Matthew to welcome the stranger.

23) Is it ever morally necessary to disobey the law to help immigrants?

There are relatively few national laws that make it necessary to disobey in order to assist immigrants. At present, there are no federal laws that must be disobeyed in order to assist immigrants.

Regardless of this fact, these laws are flawed, so there is a moral necessity to try to change them for the better.

24) To what extent should Catholics take into consideration the human aspect of the immigration?

The human aspect of immigration truly is where the issue of human dignity is found. It is human beings that migrate and not inanimate objects. Every human decision has consequences for the person who makes them and for others. So, we must strive to understand the decision making process, and the benefits and burdens and the costs to others. For the Church, immigration is ultimately a humanitarian issue because it involves the welfare of human beings. It is not just an economic, social or cultural issue, as many describe it.

25) **Even if Catholics disagree on the details, what are the elements of an immigration policy that Catholics should agree upon?**

Catholics should agree on protecting the dignity of the human person. That is the basic principle of our Catholic social teaching and everything must be guided by that teaching. Specifically, the U.S. Bishops have taken the position that the best ways to preserve human dignity are to adopt a legalization program, improve our programs for migrant workers and families, and to allow young people who were brought here as children the ability to become legalized. Attempts to deny citizenship to children born here are particularly repugnant.

26) How should Catholic immigrants be encouraged to assimilate themselves into the American way of life?

There is no question that Catholic immigrants should assimilate into the American way of life. The word assimilation, however, sometimes causes problems. Words such as acculturation and integration, perhaps, express different aspects of the same phenomenon. The fact is, immigrants after the first generation normally integrate well into American life. There are certainly exceptions, however, it does not seem that these exceptions apply to Catholic immigrants.

From our experience, we find that migrants wish to integrate, to learn English, and to understand our culture. The Church is called to help them to do that.

27) Are there any teachings of the Magisterium regarding immigration?

First, we must define the moral life in the Magisterium of the Church. The Catholic Catechism, paragraph 2032 tells us, "The Church, the "pillar and bulwark of the truth," "has received this solemn command of Christ from the apostles to announce the saving truth" (1 Tim 3:15; LG 17). "To the Church belongs the right always and everywhere to announce moral principles, including those pertaining to the social order, and to make judgments on any human affairs to the extent that they are required by the fundamental rights of the human person or the salvation of souls" (CIC, can 747§2).

The fact is, the teaching of the Magisterium goes beyond matters solely related to faith. Both the Pope and Bishops share in the ordinary teaching authority of the Church. The Roman Pontiffs of the last Century, beginning with Pius XII, have all commented on the issue of migration in one way or another. More recently, beginning with John Paul II, the annual migration message of the Holy Father has outlined various aspects of immigration policies with international perspectives. This ordinary teaching of the Magisterium is something

Catholics cannot dismiss as irrelevant to forming their consciences on this social policy issue.

28) Are there any benefits that immigrants can bring to our country?

Immigrants bring many benefits to our country. They become the new life's blood of those citizens striving to better their human condition. In doing so, they bring new energy and new diversity to a land built by immigrants. They also help our economy by working in important industries. They also can teach us much on spirituality and the worship of God.

29) Are there any benefits Catholic immigrants can bring to the Church?

The new Catholic immigrants truly can be instruments of evangelization in the Church today. Many bring a strong faith that can help transform our own Church in the United States. Immigrants to any country are usually at a crossroads between a path that will lead to the maintenance of their faith or its loss. Immigration has been called a theologizing experience in the sense that uprooting often leads people to a recognition of their true and genuine roots in God. From biblical times to now, migration has always been one of the ways that we as a people have encountered God. It is a challenge to the Church in the United States to welcome these people, to use their faith and energy for the benefit of the Church, since otherwise this new faith and energy will be lost to the Church.

30) How can the Church help Catholic immigrants remain Catholic?

The Church must assist Catholic immigrants in remaining Catholic by offering them a welcome and the opportunity first to worship in their own language with respect to their own culture, and at the same time assist them with becoming integrated into the larger Church. This is a delicate balancing act which takes generations to accomplish.

31) **Immigration is a very emotional issue. How can Catholics contribute to a more objective and fair discussion of the issue?**

Immigration, indeed, is a very emotional issue. A more objective and fair discussion of the issue would be accomplished by a wider distribution of information regarding the indisputable facts about the benefits that immigrants bring to our country. The dispelling of many myths that surround this important social phenemon is something to strive for in our country.

Catholics should seek to learn more about this issue and to listen with a critical ear to radio talk shows, cable news programs, or other negative attacks on immigrants. Catholics should be leaders in creating a civil dialogue on this important national issue.

The Shepherd's Voice Series

The Shepherd's Voice Series brings you the current teachings of Bishops and Cardinals on vital topics facing the Catholic Church today.

Catholics In the Public Square
Bishop Thomas J. Olmsted of Phoenix explains the rights and duties we Catholics have as citizens and what is and is not appropriate for us to do within the secular realm. He also describes how we should seek to influence our nation and its political processes in light of our Catholic faith.

A Will to Live: Clear Answers on End of Life Issues
Archbishop José Gomez of San Antonio, Texas, renowned expert on death-and-dying issues, explains how to approach these issues and prepare for death in a moral way, consistent with our Catholic faith.

Draw Near to Me: Heartfelt Prayers for Everyday Life
Francis Cardinal Arinze explains the power of prayer, describes how to pray, and gives examples of prayers we can use for life's triumphs and challenges. This magnificent, user-friendly work will comfort and inspire anyone seeking an ever closer relationship with the Holy Trinity.

God's Plan for You: Understanding Your Personal Vocation
With his famous vigor, Bishop Fabian Bruskewitz here gives some great tips on how to discover your vocation, deal with a conflicted heart, use Scripture in discernment, cure "vocation paralysis," or enrich and develop your vocation. Buyer, beware! You're about to get a new perspective on your life and on life in general. The bishop is out to make saints, starting with you!

What God Has Joined: A Catholic Teaching on Marriage
In this pastoral book, Bishop Kevin W. Vann explains what every Catholic needs to know about the Church's teachings on marriage and about the often confusing issues surrounding Matrimony at a time when values seem to change by the day. This booklet is essential for engaged couples, married couples, single laypersons, priests, and religious.

To order, call Basilica Press at 888-570-5182
www.basilicapress.com

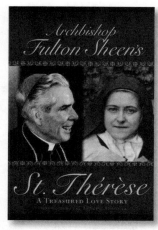

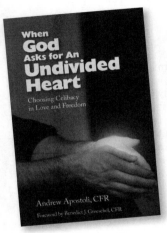